EXETER
IMPRESSIONS

EXETER
IMPRESSIONS

Robert Gambee

Hastings House, Publishers · New York

For my father
and for Uncle Ben

Library of Congress Cataloging in Publication Data
Gambee, Robert
    EXETER Impressions
    1. Exeter, N.H. — Description — Views.   2. Phillips
Exeter Academy — Pictorial works.   3. Exeter, N.H. —
History — Pictorial works.   I. Title
F44.E9G35   974.2′6   80-15841
ISBN 0-8038-1961-7

Photographic Consultation:
Peter C. Bunnell, Princeton University
Diana Mara Henry, International Center of Photography
additional photographic assistance:
Ann Bronner, Norman Krupit, Hildegard Machol
Architectural Notes by Nancy Merrill
Designed by Jacqueline Schuman
Production Supervision: Steven Borns

Printed in the United States of America by
Rapoport Printing Corp., New York

Introduction

Exeter, like any school, is a collection of the memories of those who have gone there. No matter what it may be in the present, or what changes may have occurred, it remains in the minds of the alumni(ae) the place where they first began to grow up, and to become aware of the world around them.

My very first memory of Exeter is of the station platform, on a dusty summer day: my father had taken me up to show me the school, having stipulated that if I would go to Exeter, I could then go on to whatever college I chose. My next memory is of the bright autumn foliage, when my mother left me at Cilley Hall and, her eyes glistening, drove off to the south and out of sight. I went up to Number 30 and began to unpack my trunk, as lonesome as a castaway on an Arctic ice floe. At my first meal in Dunbar Hall, where the yellow window shades were lowered against the afternoon sunlight, I wondered how I could survive until Christmas.

Things shortly became more cheerful, because the routine of the school took over, and what had been homesickness changed into a sort of nostalgia for a distant place, which could be visited on occasion but which no longer played an immediate part in my life. The immediate part was the school: the excitement of the football games, and the elation or anguish at the outcomes; the growing friendships, and the occasional, insane pleasures of "prepping around;" and the discovery — for me — of a whole new method of studying, one that depended on the student's initiative, and was rewarded in proportion to his effort. My report cards the first year were studded with D's and E's, but it wasn't for lack of trying to do better. Isolated pictures flash to mind: of Norman Hatch, balancing a piece of chalk on a yardstick while a terrified student tried to translate Caesar; of the lights going on in study hall, while the sky turned red outside; and of hockey games on the black ice upriver, with the long walk back in the fading daylight. And two sounds, never to be forgotten: the bell in the Academy Building, tolling out its sequential summons to morning chapel; and the howling whistle of the State of Maine Express, echoing over the frozen fields as the train sped southward on Friday nights.

The Exeter townspeople did not play a great part in our lives during my first years — I remember a banner over a furniture store, saying: "Ralph E. Meras Cuts Loose!" and I remember George, of George & Phillips sporting goods store, for whom I once did a poster in exchange for (I believe) a crew hat — but for the most part the Academy was our womb, and we needed no outside stimulus.

Then, senior year, five other youths and I lived in a white clapboard fraternity house on Front Street and became, in the loosest sense of the word, townspeople ourselves. We had a back yard for touch football, and a front yard for watching girls pass by in the springtime; we had neighbors, two houses down, who had a tennis court we were free to use; and we became, in short, transient members of the community. Walking to breakfast on a winter's morning, with the water on our hair turning quickly to ice, we felt almost like commuters to the Academy, and worldly well beyond our ages.

As the sign said, and I hope still says: ...UT VIRI SITIS.

Nathaniel Benchley

The Academy Library (1971)

Preface

This is a story about a town. And about a school. And about how they have coexisted for two hundred years. Their past and present are woven together; even their geographies are inseparable. The town moves up around and through the main campus of the school and beyond. Yet the school, with its vast playing fields, extends beyond the town. And no student at the school ever feels isolated from the town as he might on another campus.

The village of Exeter was first settled by a small group of farmers who wanted to live and worship according to their own religious beliefs. By the late 1700s its independent thinkers were the first in America to adopt their own constitution, set up a House of Representatives, and break away from the Crown. They also started the first paper mill in northern New England, from which sprang a publishing business that at one point was as important as the town's basic manufacturing. Finally, Exeter attracted a number of architects who merged the prosperity from the mills with the community's cultural tastes into some of the finest buildings in the state.

It is fortunate that the falls on the Squamscott River which supported Exeter's early industrialization were insufficient to sustain significant expansion. This enabled the community to maintain a balance between manufacturing, politics, and education. It was in this atmosphere that the Phillips Exeter Academy was born and grew. The position enjoyed by the Academy today among secondary schools in the world is enviable. Some say it's the best. But its long climb to excellence has not been easy and in fact was marked by periods when the very future of the Academy was in doubt. Yet today, at the end of its first 200 years, it is a strong and proud institution.

This book is divided into three sections, with the Community representing the early aspects of Exeter, the Town being a present-day view of the village, and the Academy standing on its own, but not insulated from its environment. This is the way I see Exeter.

I am most grateful to the many people who helped me in this project. Nancy Merrill deserves special recognition. Mother of six, town librarian, curator of the Exeter Historical Society, and a student for her master's degree, she nevertheless found time to go over dusty deeds and wills to provide the dates and names for the homes included here. I am also grateful to Stephen Kurtz for his strong interest in the book, supporting it from the outset and spending many hours going over its presentation. And my thanks to Paul Sadler who brought us all together in the first place.

Not every house or store or dormitory has been included. I have instead tried to create an atmosphere that is representative of the total. What I see may be different from what others see, but that, after all, is the nature of photography.

R.G.

Academy crews on the
Squamscott River

Above: The Fourth Academy Building (1915)
Opposite: The Exeter Town Hall (1855)

Above: "Gilman House," 46 Front Street (1735)
Opposite: Looking up Front Street from the Academy lawn

Above: The First Academy Building (also known as "Wells Kerr House"), 6 Tan Lane (1783)
Right: Entrance to "Bell House"
Opposite: The Academy Building Quadrangle from Main Street

Exeter, the Community

With a population of 11,000, Exeter is a small town quietly tucked away in the southeast corner of New Hampshire. It is the home of Louise's Sport Shop, Kurtz's Restaurant, and Colcord's Studebaker Garage. It is also the home of Phillips Exeter Academy. And it is where more than 200 years ago, the leaders in New Hampshire were the first in the colonies to sever their ties with England by forming their own provincial government. And after the Revolutionary War, Exeter men cast the deciding vote in favor of the new United States Constitution.

The town's beginnings are traceable to the year 1638, when the Reverend John Wheelwright and his congregation purchased a tract of land along the Squamscott River. They fled the oppressive puritanism of Massachusetts Bay and sought freedom to live and worship according to their own beliefs. It was this same motivation that later led Thomas Macy and his colleagues to leave the Massachusetts mainland and settle on Nantucket Island in 1659. The ties between these two early settlements were important in other respects as well: Exeter became a shipbuilding center and Nantucket became a major port. Much of the lumber produced at the Exeter lumber mills found its way to the island. The "Oldest House" on Nantucket, built in 1686, was a wedding present from Peter Coffin to his son and daughter-in-law, built with lumber from his Exeter mill.

The Wheelwright congregation selected a spot on the Squamscott where they thought fishing would be most productive and where nearby fields could be cleared and cultivated. The site they picked included two waterfalls, to the town's good fortune. Fish could still be trapped, but it was the exploitation of the greater potential of turning mill wheels that enabled Exeter to grow rapidly into a manufacturing center. By 1802 there were eight mills on the upper falls and three on the lower.

But Exeter was never destined to become just another New England mill town. For at the same time that Exeter was a lumber and shipbuilding center, it was also a publishing capital and the seat of government for New Hampshire. A happy by-product of this blend of prosperity and culture is architecture of a quality that was not surpassed anywhere else in the state during the eighteenth and nineteenth centuries.

The Vicar of Bilsby

John Wheelwright was born in Lincolnshire, England in 1592 and was educated at Cambridge for the ministry. He questioned certain tenets of the Church of England, which ultimately led to the revoking of his religious appointment in Bilsby and his decision to sail to America in 1636. Once in Boston, Wheelwright preached the right of every man to worship according to his own beliefs, the presence of the Holy Spirit in each individual, and the limits of the Church in enforcing conformity. Within a year Wheelwright and his

Looking down Front Street
from the Academy lawn

sister-in-law, Anne Hutchinson, who had also been preaching similar heresies, were sent packing—Anne to Rhode Island and John to New Hampshire.

Wheelwright and his congregation selected a site approximately 50 miles north of Boston just inland from the coast. They settled at the point where fresh water from the Squamscott River cascades over several rocky ledges and joins the tidal river that empties out into the Atlantic at Strawbery Banke (now Portsmouth). There were already small fishing and trading settlements at nearby Portsmouth and Dover.

A tract of land approximately 30 miles in length was purchased by Wheelwright from the Sagamore Indians, the transaction involving shirts, coats, and according to tradition, a beaver hat. The Indians were guaranteed unlimited fishing and hunting privileges. The falls in the Squamscott provided excellent fishing, but their real value was discovered a few years later—the force of the water would turn mill wheels.

Trees had to be cut down and land had to be cleared and prepared. The soil was recalcitrant and tools were scarce. But most of the settlers had emigrated from rural England and were able to make the best of the situation. There were no merchants, traders, or manufacturers among them. Few were formally educated, but they were well versed in the Scriptures and stubborn in their beliefs. Religion was taken seriously and like many other New England Puritans, they listened gladly but did not yield implicit faith. They questioned, reasoned, picked things apart and, when through, held to strong convictions.

The community was originally called the "Church at Exeter." At first the land was held in common but then individual allocations were made. About two dozen families founded the original community, some having been part of Wheelwright's following in Massachusetts and others arriving directly from England. Those arriving in Boston who indicated friendship for Wheelwright were allowed to stay a few weeks before being told to move on.

By 1640 the population of Exeter numbered more than 100. In that year, one of their members, Thomas Wilson, built a grist mill on the small island separating the Squamscott falls. By 1648 the village permitted a more significant development to occur. Edward Gilman, who had come to Exeter the year before, took advantage of the area's abundance of pine trees and erected the first saw mill. This enabled the town to tap what was to prove its greatest resource, timber, and started Exeter on its path toward industrial prosperity.

When New Hampshire was united with Massachusetts in 1643, Wheelwright realized that his views would no longer be in favor and moved on to Maine. Without steady leadership Exeter foundered until 1650, when the Reverend Samuel Dudley was appointed to the church. He stayed until his death in 1683 at the age of 73 and, together with Edward Gilman, he is credited with Exeter's early survival. For Dudley was not only a minister, but a farmer and a sound businessman.

In 1680 Charles II decided to split up New Hampshire and Massachusetts and appointed a new Governor of New Hampshire with the power to rule without an Assembly. The inhabitants met this turn of events with measured outrage. While they had respect for authority, they were not about to give up freely what they had worked so hard to carve out of the wilderness. Nor were they willing to pay taxes without their consent. This, it must be remembered, occurred a hundred years before the Revolution! There was cause for further outrage when Governor Cranfield, the representative of the Crown, established laws against trespassing in pine forests marked for masts for His Majesty's Navy.

But with the Glorious Revolution of 1689 in England and the accession of William and Mary, New Hampshire's future continued to be uncertain. The possibility of returning to

Massachusetts loomed large again. Peter Coffin and John Gilman were Exeter's representatives at further conferences called to consider reuniting the two colonies.

Gilman built his house at 12 Water Street about 1680 *(24, 25)*. The original structure was well adapted for protection against Indian raids. The first attack on the town had occurred in 1675, and they continued until 1723. There was never a general attack, but there were frequent ambushes and massacres. Gilman had his home constructed as a garrison, with heavy squared logs forming the walls and an overhanging second story from which arrows and hot liquids could be dropped on unwanted callers. The logs were sawed rather than simply hewn, and they were fitted together in massive dovetailed joints.

John Gilman's grandson Peter was also a councilor, and he made significant changes to the house in 1772 *(32, 33)*. The Governor of New Hampshire at the time was John Wentworth, a gentleman who enjoyed a certain amount of ceremony. The large front wing was added with him in mind, as was the upstairs bedroom for his overnight visits. The windows of the house were enlarged, the walls clapboarded on the outside and plastered on the inside. In 1793 the house was sold to Ebenezer Clifford, and while he lived there, young Daniel Webster came to board for several months in 1796 during his enrollment at the Academy.

Another early Exeter home is the one built around 1675 by Edward Sewall on the Epping Road *(23)*. Land was granted to him by the community with the understanding he would build a house on it and not use the land for cultivation alone. Like Gilman's garrison, the Sewall home was built for protection against Indians. The walls have heavy planking on the outside and are bricked inside. During extensive remodelling in subsequent years, bullets were found imbedded in the bricks.

But not all the homes built at this time were fortresslike. Francis Lyford's homestead of 1681 *(23)* was a building more typical of settled communities than frontier towns. Lyford was probably too busy to worry about occasional Indian raids anyway — he was a farmer (he sold saltmarsh hay to the Exeter lumbermen for their horses), a ship captain (he transported lumber from Exeter to Boston and points south), and later a weaver.

Although Exeter was located at the head of the tidal basin of the Squamscott and had direct access to the Atlantic, shipbuilding rather than commercial shipping itself became an important occupation for the community. Begun in the mid-1600s, shipbuilding was flourishing in the 1760s. Vessels of up to 500 tons were launched for trade along the coast to the West Indies and to Europe. Six to eight vessels were usually completed each season, although at the industry's peak 22 were said to be under various stages of construction.

Perhaps one reason why Exeter went after shipbuilding and manufacturing so seriously was the realization by the mid-1700s that timber was not in an endless supply. Merely cutting trees or logs was not yielding the necessary financial reward that the community leaders felt was required. Furthermore, pure lumbering was not an occupation to be encouraged. It required little mental ability and great physical strength, which often culminated in exhaustion and heavy drinking. The taverns were popular with the lumbering community and were scenes of riots against the Crown's various mast tree regulations for the Royal Navy.

The fresh water Exeter River cascades over two falls and
becomes the Squamscott River. The first mill was built
here in 1640.

Above: The placid Exeter River just above the first fall
Right: The Exeter powder house (1771). Gunpowder
produced by Samuel Hobart's mill was stored here
during the Revolutionary War. It is the oldest structure
of its kind in the region.
Opposite: The Edward Sewall House, 16 Epping Road
(ca. 1675) and The Francis Lyford House, Newmarket
Road (ca. 1681)

Opposite: The John Gilman House (also known as the "Gilman Garrison"), 12 Water Street (ca. 1680; 1772)
Above: The window desk used by Daniel Webster in the "Gilman Garrison."

Edward Gilman built the first saw mill in 1648 and followed it with a second one in 1650. The town obligingly made certain that no one else could build mills in such a way as to hinder his operations. By the end of the next century Exeter had two dams on the falls, providing water power for four double-geared corn mills, four saw mills, two oil mills (for obtaining linseed oil from flaxseed) and a fulling mill (for shrinking wool cloth). By 1777 Exeter boasted the first paper mill in northern New England, established by Richard Jordan. This mill was an important addition because paper was often in such short supply that many newspapers were forced to suspend publication and then start up again at a later time.

But not all the mills were for industrial merchandise. Exeter also had one snuff mill and two chocolate mills.

A Feeling of Independence

Exeter was becoming a hub of prosperity and importance in the region. By the third quarter of the eighteenth century, it was the capital of New Hampshire and was playing a critical role in events leading up to the Revolution. On December 15, 1774, 25 citizens led by Nathaniel Folsom and Nicholas Gilman *(12, 37, 42)* made an early morning raid on Fort William and Mary at the entrance of Portsmouth harbor, taking gunpowder and guns back to Exeter for future use. This raid and another led by John Sullivan of Durham at the same time are considered the first aggressive acts of the American Revolution. In January of that year a resolution had been adopted almost unanimously at the town meeting, declaring that "we are ready, on all necessary occasions, to risk our lives and fortunes in defense of our rights and liberties."

On April 19, 1775, the day the British sent their troops from Boston to Concord, word of the battle reached Exeter by the late afternoon. It was confirmed by a second report from Haverill later that night. The town mobilized every available man into a battalion and by nine o'clock the following morning over a hundred men were on their way, by foot, to Lexington.

As capital of the Province of New Hampshire, Exeter was the scene of several provincial congresses convened in 1774 and 1775. From this body is supposed to have come the first suggestion to the Continental Congress for independence from England. For at this point the Royal Governor of New Hampshire had left for England and the people were without a leader. On December 21, 1775, the Provincial Congress decided that New Hampshire needed its own government. As a result, a House of Representatives was established and a written constitution was drawn up.

The constitution had many flaws, but it worked primarily because the people of Exeter and the rest of New Hampshire were industrious and serious enough to make it succeed. With its signing on January 5, 1776, New Hampshire, under the leadership of the men at Exeter, became the first American colony to assert its right to govern itself—and thereby the first to break away from England. The news of the Declaration of Independence did not reach Exeter until July 16, 1776.

Exeter had thus emerged as the center of activity in the state from a civil, legislative, and military viewpoint. The town was most proud of its role, which in retrospect seems disproportionate to its size at the time—the population was only 1,741! Not only was New Hampshire the first state in the new Union to adopt its own constitution, but in June 1788 it cast the deciding vote in favor of the Federal constitution—an act that bound the original 13 states together as a republic.

After the war for independence was over, George Washington toured the new nation and decided to pay a visit to Exeter. It was announced well in advance that he would visit Folsom's Tavern on November 4, 1789 *(43)*. What he did not make clear was that he would be there for breakfast, and his early arrival caught the special color guard unprepared and made the general welcoming ceremonies somewhat chaotic.

The tavern Washington visited was built by Colonel Samuel Folsom in 1775. The original Folsom had come to Exeter from England in 1648 and worked in the lumbering business with his brother-in-law John Gilman of the "Gilman Garrison" *(24)*. On November 18, 1783, a group of Revolutionary officers met in the tavern to form the New Hampshire chapter of the Society of the Cincinnati—named after Lucius Cincinnatus, a Roman who became a leader in defending his city at the time of an invasion and then, when the mission was accomplished, returned to farming. The founders of the Society were officers in the American army who were "taken from the citizens of their country" and returned to civilian status after the war. The Society subsequently purchased the "Ladd-Gilman" House on Water Street *(36-38)*, which now serves as its regional headquarters. (Today some of the early houses in Exeter are referred to by names that include owners other than the original builders. These are referred to in quotation marks.)

Nine years after Washington caught Exeter asleep, two young men from Boston drove into town late in the evening. They had trouble getting a room because the inn was full and everyone else had gone to bed. Realizing that memories of the President's last visit were still strong, the two visitors decided to mention to those still in residence at the bar of the tavern that President Adams was coming to Exeter that night and would be arriving very shortly indeed. They had ridden ahead from Haverill to give an advance warning. Soon every household was awake in haste to prepare for the President's reception. The Bostonians found lodgings in a house whose owners had been awakened and they were shortly snug in bed. The rest of the town waited and waited for President Adams, who was also snug in bed—but in New York.

Exeter Architecture

Most of the houses along Front Street and in the "Plains Area" of Exeter were built before the Revolution. The oldest one on Front Street is the John Lord House, built around 1725 *(34)*. Its first owner was a deacon of the Second Church. Amos Tuck later lived in the house from 1840 until 1853, when he built a home at 89 Front Street *(69)*. His son, Edward, was a benefactor of Dartmouth College. A similar house was built about 1730 by Daniel Thing at 76 Front Street *(35)*. (Like several homes in town, this one had many lives—serving first as a tavern and then as a fraternity house for Phillips Exeter Academy.) The house was also occupied by Benjamin Lovering, who was a cobbler along with his sons Ben, Richard, and John. Young Ben built the house at 66 Front Street *(61)* and Richard lived close by at 64 Front Street, where "Knight House" presently stands *(60)*. The senior Lovering married Sarah Swasey, whose family has been a long-standing one in Exeter. It includes Ambrose Swasey, the co-founder of Warner and Swasey Corporation and the donor of the Swasey Bandstand Pavilion *(77)* and Parkway *(2)*. His birthplace is now called "Fort Rock Farm" and is presently the home of his niece, Leona Henderson, and her husband, Warren *(72, 73)*.

The minister of the First Church, Woodbridge Odlin, built the house across Front Street, No. 79, about 1750. It was originally next to the Academy's "Gilman House"; bay windows and a Victorian porch were added at a later date *(35)*.

The magnificent house at the corner of Water Street and Governor's Lane, presently owned by the Society of the Cincinnati, was built by Nathaniel Ladd in 1721 *(36-38)*. When he moved to Portsmouth in 1747 he sold the house to his brother-in-law, Daniel Gilman, and hence it is commonly referred to today as the "Ladd-Gilman House." Daniel's son Nicholas was the first treasurer of New Hampshire and was considered to be the "brains of the Revolution in New Hampshire." Nicholas made substantial alterations to the house in 1752, including covering its brick walls with clapboards (the maintenance cost of which continues to exceed the original expense by an ever-climbing geometric progression).

Nicholas Gilman later bought the house at 46 Front Street *(12, 43)* that Dr. Dudley Odlin built about 1735. His son, Nathaniel Gilman, was also a state treasurer and active in public service. Nathaniel lived in the house until his death in 1862. His widow then married Charles H. Bell, Governor of New Hampshire, U.S. Senator, and a noted historian. The house was purchased by the Phillips Exeter Academy in 1905 and is now the home of its Principal, Stephen G. Kurtz.

The gambrel roof and double chimneys of this house are similar to those of the 1723 "Odiorne-Bickford House" at 25 Cass Street *(39)* and the 1750 Eliphalet Giddinge House at 77 Park Street *(41)*. Both of these buildings were also called double houses because of the twin chimneys and central hallway. Their construction marks a break from the earlier central chimney style as represented by the Benjamin Philbrick House at 70 Park Street, which dates from about 1715. The house at 25 Cass Street was built by Major John Gilman whose son-in-law, Deacon Thomas Odiorne, was a country trader. He and his wife operated a shop in a corner of the house and sold tea, sugar, and general merchandise. A spring house was built later in the yard offering fresh water to "subscribers." The house may have served as a stop for escaping slaves on the underground railway during the Civil War. They probably came up from the river and hid in a warm closet behind the chimney and under the stairs.

Around the corner at 18 Green Street was Thomas Odiorne's canvas factory *(47)*, which dates from 1790. It was the first such operation in New Hampshire. According to the testimony of sea captains, Odiorne's duck wore well, was free of mildew, and was as good as any imported fabric. Next door was the home and shop of Deacon James Burley, a cabinet maker, *(47)* also built about 1790.

The house at 77 Park Street was built by Colonel Eliphalet Giddinge for his son Nathaniel. It was purchased in 1809 by Jeremiah Smith, who previously had rented the 1770 "Lee-Wetherell House" at 41 Front Street *(44)*, moved in from the "Plains" around 1798. Jeremiah Smith was a lawyer, Governor of New Hampshire, Congressman, U.S. District Attorney, and Chief Justice of the New Hampshire Superior Court. He and his son were influential citizens.

Eliphalet Giddinge was the son of Zebulon Giddinge, who built the tavern at 37 Park Street *(40)* in 1723. It was conveniently situated on the hill where the lumbermen hauled their logs down to the river. Afterwards they came back up the hill to drink. And drinking was a favorite entertainment. In 1734 a group assembled at Zebulon's tavern to protest the new regulation that all pine trees with a diameter greater than two feet had to be reserved for masts for the King's ships. Some of His Majesty's representatives were in town from Portsmouth to inspect the saw mills and were refreshing themselves at another tavern. The Exeter men stormed in there and tossed them out into the streets, but only after knocking a few holes in their boats. It was a dreary trip back to Portsmouth.

The hipped roof of Giddinge's Tavern was duplicated elsewhere in Exeter. It is visible on Folsom's Tavern in a more elevated style *(43)* and on the Theophilus Smith House *(48)*. The latter has twin chimneys like the "Jeremiah Smith House" *(41)*, both built about 1750, yet the "Lewis Cass House," also from 1750, retains the central chimney *(40)*. The Cass House at 11 Cass Street (originally called Cross Street) was built by Theophilus Gilman. His son-in-law was Major Jonathan Cass, a successful Revolutionary officer and blacksmith. Jonathan's son, Lewis Cass, was Secretary of War, Territorial Governor, and Democratic candidate for President in 1848.

The central chimney design continued to be popular in the next few years, as indicated by the Samuel Dutch House at 33 Main Street *(45)* built in 1760, the Eliphalet Hale House at 41 Main Street *(46)* built in 1755, and the Ephraim Robinson House at 336 Water Street *(46)* built in 1766. The last was one of eleven houses where gunpowder was hidden after that celebrated raid on Fort William and Mary in 1774.

A central chimney often contained up to seven or eight fireplaces. The one in the Benjamin Folsom House at 171 High Street *(43)*, built in 1740, rests on two large barrel vaults in the cellar. They have hardly settled at all in 250 years despite the tremendous weight according to historian Henry Bragdon, the present owner. The fireplaces are high and shallow, throwing off heat remarkably well. Another house with a central chimney is the 1763 Josiah Gilman House at 39 Front Street *(52)*. Its style departs from the square box design in order to conform more to the narrowness of its plot along Front Street. And since it is so close to the street, it is possible to see more fully how the house has aged — sagging a bit here and there with hardly a shutter or windowsill running in a straight line. Benjamin Gilman subsequently lived here. In 1797 he teamed up with an architect named Bradbury Johnson to form the Exeter Aqueduct Company. They laid a system of hollowed logs under Front Street and nearby streets, at a pitch, in order to convey fresh spring water by gravity to "subscribers." The aqueduct was another Exeter first, and the company was incorporated by the State of New Hampshire in 1801. The two also collaborated on similar fresh water systems in Boston, Portsmouth, Salem, and New London.

Bradbury Johnson and his partner, Ebenezer Clifford, helped turn Exeter into a distinctive architectural center. As the local mills enriched Exeter during the last years of the eighteenth century, Johnson and Clifford made sure that nothing of quiet beauty or intellectual excellence was sacrificed during the rush to industrialize. In 1794 they designed the Second Academy Building for Phillips Exeter Academy (unfortunately, no longer standing). Its design was of such unusual refinement that the president of Yale said it was superior to any other academic building he had ever seen.

A few years later, the partners also built the house for Dr. Samuel Tenney *(50)* which is now located at 65 High Street, having been moved in 1893 from a spot near the Congregational Church. The house has fine proportions and boasts a raised central clerestory, tall chimneys, and a tasteful doorway. And Tenney, a successful surgeon, co-founder of the Exeter Social Library, and an author of papers on medicine, politics, and law, was an uncommon enough man to demand such a house.

Johnson and Clifford also designed the Congregational Church, which was built between 1798 and 1800 *(74, 93)*. The church had open seating, with men on one side and women on the other. There were only three box pews—sold at auction to the highest bidders. In 1838 substantial changes were made inside but the exterior was fortunately left alone. The church's proportions and classical detail represent one of New England's best expressions of post-Revolutionary architecture. It drew admirers from all over the region, including a few who were interested in copying it. The Congregational Church was once called the "First Parish" and its members descend from the original congregation of John Wheelwright.

It is possible that Johnson and Clifford also had a hand in the design of Josiah Coffin Smith's house at 27 High Street *(49)* built in 1789. Josiah grew up next door at 25 High Street in the house built by his father, Theophilus, in about 1750. His father was prominent in the colonists' efforts to stop paying taxes imposed by the Crown. Theophilus Smith, Jr. built the house at 16 High Street around 1776 *(48)* (note the "nine-over-six" windows). Josiah had three sons and three daughters. In later years he would visit all of their households daily to find out what each was serving for dinner and then choose to eat where his tastes led him.

The three Federal-style houses at 4, 12, and 14 Front Street *(52)* were built between 1809 and 1826. They are of three stories and were considered easier to heat and more economical to build because less foundation and roof area were needed.

No. 4 *(59)* was built by George Sullivan in 1809. He became a State Attorney General and then a U.S. Senator. The house was later purchased by the Sleeper family, who were jewelers in Exeter for almost a hundred years. The house at No. 14 *(58)* was built in 1815. It was purchased shortly thereafter for about $3,000 by Dr. William Perry, who was the main doctor in the Exeter community for over 50 years. (His son followed in his footsteps by practicing for almost 60 years himself.) Dr. Perry put a stove in place of the open hearth and also introduced another new item to Exeter—the bathtub. Perry's son-in-law, Albertus Dudley, bought the house later.

John Gardner built No. 12 Front Street in 1826 *(57)*. The cost was high for the time: $6,963, including rum and board for the crew (the bill includes $31.80 for 53 gallons of rum). The house has remained in the Gardner family to this day. John Gardner came to Exeter in the late 1700s, married, and joined his father-in-law in the hardware business. This store still carries on the business, originally established in 1770 *(85)*.

At 60 Front Street is the Academy Admissions Office *(59)*. The earliest section of this house was built in 1808 by Captain Epes Ellery and was originally located at the edge of town. He was a retired sea captain and soon tired of farming. He also found it too quiet where he was, so in the winter of 1811 he put the house on sleds and moved it across the frozen fields to its present location. John Rogers bought the house in 1816 and, in the practice of the time, added an enlarged and impressive front to the older home. The widow of James Bell, a U.S. Senator, moved in with her daughters in 1860. Mrs. Bell remodeled the house extensively in the 1890s, even blocking out two front windows because they let in too much light. Other houses on Front Street underwent similar Victorian "improvements."

Benjamin Lovering, Jr. built the handsome three-story house at 66 Front Street around 1820 *(61)*. It has an unusual "fan light" over the door *(56)*. In 1830 his brother built a home at 64 Front Street, where the present "Knight House" stands. The latter now serves as an Academy dormitory.

When Dr. Benjamin Abbot was head of the Academy, he had the house at 81 Front

Street built as a wedding gift for his daughter Elizabeth and her new husband, Dr. David Gorham, in 1824 *(61)*. At first Gorham's office was in the house but after his bride's complaints of constant medical odors, he was moved out into the yard. The adjacent doctor's office is a miniature duplicate of the main house, with a large shuttered fan light in the pediment, smooth boards on the front of the house, and regular clapboards on the sides *(61)*.

The pattern of smoothed fronts and clapboard sides was duplicated in the pair of Greek Revival houses at 40 Front Street and 60 Main Street *(64, 65)*. The first was built by Alfred Conner in 1840 for his brother Charles. The second was built for himself in 1843 as a slightly bigger twin. (Note the unusual sunburst fence.) The front walls are 17 inches thick. Alfred Connor also built the Amos Tuck House *(69)* and Abbot Hall, the Academy's first dormitory *(118, 174)*.

Abbot Hall was built in 1855. Before then, those students unable to afford housing in town were put up in "Williams House," which the school acquired and modified in 1850 *(65)*. This building was originally built around 1825 and housed the offices and printing operations of the J. and B. Williams brothers. John Williams opened a publishing house in 1818 and his brother Benjamin, a bookbinder, joined him shortly thereafter. The business flourished for about 20 years. John built a home at 80 Front Street in 1828. His brother built a twin on Ladd's Lane the same year *(66, 67)*. The bookbindery was located in the back of Benjamin's house. John died in 1845 at the age of 48, leaving a wife and five children. His brother "fell into bad habits" and the business folded soon after.

Other interesting brick buildings from this period include the Granite Bank at 27 Front Street *(68)*. Built in 1831, it had living quarters for a cashier upstairs. It is now the home of the Exeter Historical Society.

Across the street is Gorham Hall, built in 1851 on the site of the Squamscott House. This building, originally a hotel, is owned by the Academy and is named after a former trustee, Dr. David Gorham *(122)*. New Hampshire believes that Amos Tuck founded the Republican Party on the premises on October 12, 1853, although the claim is disputed by the people of Jackson, Michigan. Nevertheless, Tuck was involved with bringing Abraham Lincoln to Exeter in 1860 to see his son, then a student at the Academy. He was taking a year at Exeter to prepare for Harvard, having been unsuccessful at being admitted his first time around. They had dinner where Robert was living at 7 Pleasant Street *(68)* and the father spent the night. Lincoln gave a speech at Exeter and in a few other New England towns on his way home. One reason Lincoln received the Republican Presidential nomination was because the enthusiastic following he had generated on this trip had been noticed and approved by members of his party. Both Lincoln and his son benefitted from their Exeter visits; Robert got into Harvard and his father eventually got into the White House.

The front wing added to the "Gilman Garrison" in 1772,
showing the room where the Governor's Council met
(above) and the bedroom where the Governor stayed
when the Council was in session *(opposite)*

Above: The John Lord House, 72 Front Street (ca. 1725) — the oldest house on Front Street
Opposite: The Daniel Thing House, 76 Front Street (ca. 1730) and the Woodbridge Odlin House, 79 Front Street (ca. 1750)

Above: The Nathaniel Ladd House (also known as the "Ladd-Gilman House" or "Cincinnati Memorial Hall"), Governor's Lane (1721; 1752)
Opposite: The Long Parlor and the Tap Room of the "Ladd-Gilman House"

Above: The Lt. Joseph Mills Room and the Daniel
Webster Room in the "Ladd-Gilman House." Joseph
Mills was President of the Society of the Cincinnati
from 1799 to 1809. Daniel Webster stayed with the
Gilmans when he came back to Exeter as a Circuit Judge.
Opposite: The John Gilman House (also known as the
"Odiorne-Bickford House"), 25 Case Street (ca. 1723),
from the outside and a view of its original kitchen

39

Opposite: Zebulon Giddinge's Tavern, 37 Park Street (ca. 1723) and the Theophilus Gilman House (also known as the "Lewis Cass House"), 11 Cass Street (ca. 1750)

Above: The Eliphalet Giddinge House (also known as the "Jeremiah Smith House"), 77 Park Street (ca. 1750)

Above: The Dudley Odlin House (also known as "Gilman House"), 46 Front Street (ca. 1735). The tall clock in the front hall was made by Levi and Abel Hutchins in Concord around 1788.

Opposite: The Benjamin Folsom House, 171 High Street (1740) and Samuel Folsom's Tavern, 21 Spring Street (1775)

Opposite: The "Lee-Wetherell House," 41 Front Street (ca. 1770)
Above: The John Lougee House, 65 Front Street (ca. 1778) and the Samuel Dutch House, 33 Main Street (1760)

Above: The Eliphalet Hale House, 41 Main Street (1760) and the Ephraim Robinson House, 336 Water Street (1766)
Opposite: The James Burley House, 22 Green Street (ca. 1790) and Thomas Odiorne's canvas factory, 18 Green Street (ca. 1790)

Opposite: The Theophilus Smith House, 25 High Street (ca. 1750) and the Theophilus Smith, Jr. House, 16 High Street (ca. 1776)
Above: The Josiah Coffin Smith House, 27 High Street (1789)

Above: The Nathaniel Conner House, 330 Water Street (1800) and the Samuel Tenney House, 65 High Street (ca. 1798)

Opposite: "Doctor's House," 16 Tan Lane (ca. 1796)

Opposite: The Josiah Gilman House, 39 Front Street
(ca. 1763) and the Sullivan, Gardner, and Perry Houses
on Front Street (1809, 1826, and 1815)
Above: The Oliver Towle House (also known as "Veazey
House"), 25 Main Street (1811)

Above: Looking up Main Street past the Josiah Batchelder House, 3
Main Street (1834) and a house he later built for his daughter, 7
Main Street (1850)
Opposite: The Winthrop Dow House, 75 Front Street (1886)

Above: Doorways of the Lovering House and Bell House
Opposite: The John Gardner House, 12 Front Street (1826)

56

Opposite: The William Perry House, (also known as the "Perry-Dudley House"), 14 Front Street (1815)
Above: The Epes Ellery House (also known as "Bell House"), 60 Front Street (1808; 1816)
Right: The George Sullivan House (also known as the "Sullivan-Sleeper House"), 4 Front Street (1809)

Above: "Knight House," 64 Front Street (ca. 1830)
Opposite, top: The Benjamin Lovering, Jr. House, 66
Front Street (ca. 1820); *bottom:* The David Gorham
House, 81 Front Street (ca. 1824) and Dr. Gorham's office

Above: The Samuel Colcord House, 101 Main Street
(ca. 1809)
Opposite: The Shadrach Drew House (also known as
"Barrett House" or "Lamont House"), 10 Tan Lane (ca. 1838)

Left: The Charles Conner House, 40 Front Street (1840)
Opposite: The Alfred Conner House, 60 Main Street (1843) and "Williams House," the original home of the J. and B. Williams publishing business and later the Academy's first dormitory, 17 Spring Street (1825)

Above: The John Williams House, 80 Front Street (1828)
Right: The bindery operations were located in this building which adjoins the Benjamin Williams House
Opposite: The Benjamin Williams House (also known as "Anderson House"), Ladd's Lane (1828)

Above: The Charles Folsom House, 7 Pleasant Street (ca. 1830) and the Simeon Folsom House, 8 High Street (1816)
Right: The Granite Bank (now home of the Exeter Historical Society), 27 Front Street (1831)
Opposite, top: The Amos Tuck House, 89 Front Street (1853); *bottom:* The Theodore K. Mace House (also known as the "Mace-Merrill House"), 112 Front Street (1856; 1879)

Above: The Alva Wood House (also known as "Pearl House"), 84 Front Street (1864) and the Henry C. Moses House, One Pine Street (1868)
Opposite: The Charles Burley House (also known as the "Schute House"), 3 Pine Street (ca. 1860)

"Fort Rock Farm," birthplace of Ambrose Swasey, on Newmarket Road. The house was built about 1790 and was purchased by Nathaniel Swasey in 1838. The Ebenezer Swasey House (ca. 1763) is still standing next door *(opposite, bottom)*.

Exeter, the Town

To say that Exeter is a mill town is misleading. Yes, it had mills and it had them early. There were saw and grist mills. But there was also a paper mill—the first in that part of the country. Having a ready source of paper enabled those in Exeter who were interested in education to launch a sizeable printing and publishing business. The first newspaper, the *Exeter Morning Chronicle*, was started in 1775. By 1790 two book publishers had opened their doors, starting businesses that provided an important counterweight to milling and manufacturing.

The fortunes of the town's various newspapers rose and fell for several years until 1831 when John Sleeper founded the *Exeter News Letter*, which continues today. Another important newspaper was established in 1878. It was *The Exonian*, the first newspaper ever published by students at an independent secondary school.

And the manufacturing went on. The restless and innovative Dr. Perry set up a mill in 1824 to produce starch from potatoes—a cheaper and more effective sizing material than British gum. The starch was sold to the cotton mills in Lowell and it was quite a successful operation until it was copied elsewhere. In 1830 a mill was built by the Exeter Manufacturing Company to produce cotton sheeting. It has remained in continuous operation since then, even during the blackest days of the 1930s, when so many others were closed down. Today the mill is owned by the Clemson Fabrics division of Milliken & Company.

In 1884 the Exeter Building Association was formed to raise funds for a manufacturing center to be constructed at the other end of town from the mills. Subscriptions of stock were offered for sale to leading businessmen. It soon became quite a cooperative effort, with the Gilman family donating the land, another offering to provide bricks, and the entire town being encouraged to come to a fund-raising gala opening. After the four story building was finished but before the machinery was put in, the opening party was given. An elaborate dinner was served on the first floor and there was roller skating on the second and third floors and dancing to the Tilton orchestra on the fourth. The Exeter Boot and Shoe Company began operation after the streamers were swept up, followed by the Wise Shoe Company, and presently by the research and development division of Nike Incorporated, manufacturers of athletic shoes. One of the current employees is the fourth generation in his family to have worked in the plant. Another puts in a full day at the age of 83 and frequently brings vegetables from his garden or home-made fudge for everyone.

Exeter became known for other crafts besides shoe manufacturing during the late 1700s and early 1800s. Hat makers, cabinet makers, and silversmiths flourished, and there was such a leather tanning business that the south side of the Academy yard is bordered by Tan Lane. At one point Exeter was the leading manufacturer of saddles throughout the Eastern states.

Exeter's reputation as a thriving manufacturing center and a place of refinement created

The Congregational Church (1798; 1838)

an atmosphere in which Phillips Exeter Academy was able to grow and thrive. For the Academy was a product of the same environment that produced the leading merchants, manufacturers, publishers, and statesmen.

To balance the boys' academy, William Robinson, a local resident who became successful in the cotton trade, left funds to start the Robinson Female Seminary when he died in 1864. The school was run by the town and was tuition-free to any girl of Exeter. Girls who came from elsewhere in New England were charged $40.00. In 1955 the town voted to have a co-educational high school, and the Seminary was used for other purposes. It was boarded up in 1961 and shortly thereafter succumbed to a disastrous fire.

Today the town of Exeter, no longer a hub of trade or politics, is more quiet than in earlier years. For the inhabitants, life goes on in its individual industrious ways — no one is sitting back, fat and happy with the past. In many respects it is fortunate that the area's growth came so early and was fully played out by the time larger mill and manufacturing centers had begun to thrive. Exeter's decline in political and economic importance has preserved the town's architectural integrity as a smaller community and one in harmony with its principal tenant, Phillips Exeter Academy.

The Exeter Town Hall (1855) and the Swasey Pavilion (1916)

Above: Looking up Water Street, the town's business district
Opposite: The Merrill Block (1873)

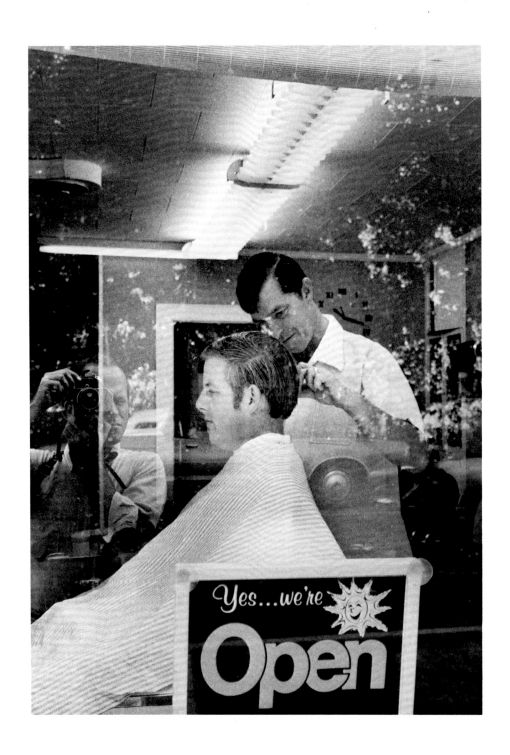

Signs and services don't change very much

There are only two "chain stores" on Water Street.
These are some of the "independents."

Exeter has a drug store, a movie theatre and several
hardware stores. Kimball's was started in 1770.

Ben's Photo Shop is up-to-date; Moore's Shoe Store was last remodeled in 1926; and Batchelder's Book Store was originally established in 1829.

Above: The Phillips Exeter Academy Book Store on
Spring Street
Opposite: The Baptist Church on Spring and Front
Streets, designed by Peabody & Stearns of Boston and
built in 1875

Opposite: Inside the Methodist Church on Front Street, built by the Universalist Society in 1845
Above: Inside Phillips Church, originally built as the Second Congregational Church in 1898 and purchased by Phillips Exeter Academy in 1922

 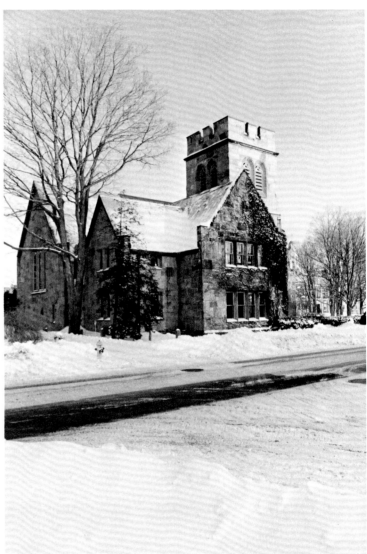

The Methodist Church, Phillips Church, and the Congregational Church

Opposite, top: A wedding at St. Michael's Catholic Church; *bottom:* Christ Episcopal Church.
Above: Gale Park and a wedding party next to Daniel Chester French's War Memorial

The Squamscott River and the Exeter Manufacturing
Company building (1830), presently owned by the
Clemson Fabrics division of Milliken & Company

Above: The Exeter Handkerchief Company's Remnant Store
Opposite: The Exeter Boot & Shoe Company building (1894),
presently owned by Nike Incorporated

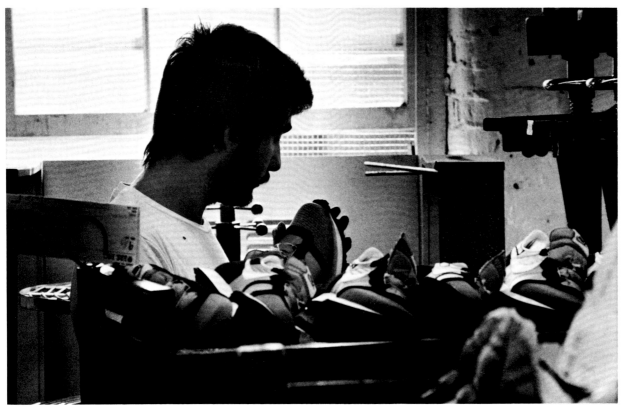

Employees of the Research and Development
division of Nike Incorporated

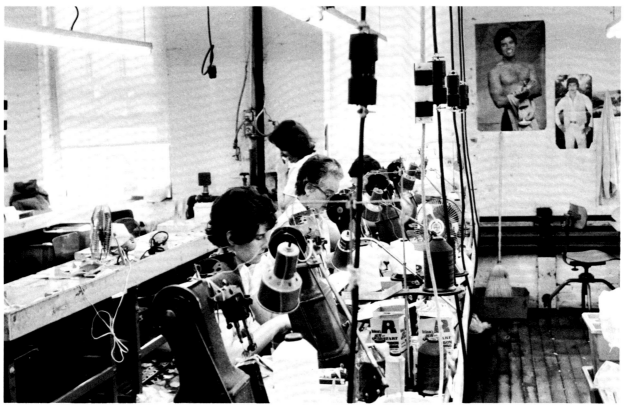

Exeter, the Academy

So in the fall father and I went East. At first I was a little vexed that he felt it necessary to come, but as the train from Boston neared Exeter I was awfully glad that he was beside me. I got more and more nervous as we came closer and closer to the Unknown. There were loud laughing groups who seemed contemptuous of me, a new boy. Father understood this and tried to encourage me with pats on the knee. I had a moment of real panic as the train came to a stop in the station, but it was too late now to retreat.

Donald Ogden Stewart '12
Author

A century ago a young man who spoke of "going to Exeter" meant he was intending to visit the well-known New Hampshire town. Today that same statement implies something else: attendance at Phillips Exeter Academy. The school has long enjoyed an enviable reputation for scholastic excellence and leaves a lasting mark upon its graduates, because of its high educational standards and because of the impressionable age (14 to 18) at which students are exposed to them. There is something special about attending a school that by almost every measurement ranks at the top academically. It is not a school for everyone, for its atmosphere can be heady.

Exeter's leadership in education is largely due to the care its faculty devotes to a student's moral and intellectual growth. Thanks to the generosity of Edward Harkness in the 1930s, the classes of a dozen students are conducted around large oval tables. At Exeter there are no back rows to drowse in. A Harkness classroom provides one of the lowest student to faculty ratios found anywhere in the United States. Furthermore, most faculty members are required to coach a sport in the afternoon and reside in dormitory apartments. The interaction of students and teachers is constant. Perhaps because of its high standards and its unusual approach to maintaining them, the Academy instills a measure of overconfidence in its graduates. That is achieved, however, only near the end of the program. Certainly the incoming 14- or 15-year old who faces grading standards largely unknown elsewhere has little reason for arrogance. Accounts written by alumni of the most varied backgrounds and experience reveal a common theme: they learned self-confidence through early experience with adversity. For no matter how gifted a student may be in one area, the Academy manages to sprinkle a healthy dose of setbacks among the successes, not out of design or malice, but out of a conviction that young people can withstand the rigors of hard work.

Those who do well—and the great majority do—sense the support of the school behind

The Fourth Academy Building (1915)

them. Confidence grows, and by the senior year they have been admitted into demanding colleges and universities. Exeter turns out strong individuals, a good many independent thinkers, and few followers.

The Phillipses

The idea of founding an academy open to "youth from all quarters" grew out of the experiences of Samuel Phillips during the American Revolution. He was a sixth-generation descendent of Puritan founders of Andover, Massachusetts, and he possessed the determination and seriousness of mind that such an inheritance implies. At the age of 26, Sam Phillips had already achieved a place of honor in Massachusetts society. He was politically active and successful in his investments, the cornerstone of them being a gunpowder plant that had hastily been built to supply Washington's army during the siege of Boston. He remained troubled by the inadequacy of training available to the young men around him, and he was highly critical of the education he had received at the Governor Dummer Academy in Byfield and at Harvard. The experiment in republican government would demand responsible, disciplined leaders of a quality no American school could promise to produce. What more worthy undertaking could there be than to found and nurture a secondary school on new lines emphasizing self-reliance and religious piety? Lacking enough money to finance the undertaking, he turned to his uncle, John Phillips of nearby Exeter, New Hampshire. By 1778 Phillips Academy at Andover had opened its doors, and three years later John Phillips directed even larger portions of his ample fortune to the establishment of an academy on similar lines in the town of Exeter. Other academies sprang up throughout New England, but none were as carefully nurtured as the two Phillips Academies, which remained under private sponsorship long after others had become tax-supported public schools.

Both Phillipses were deeply religious men of the Calvinist stripe who were preoccupied with man's final destination. John Phillips, merchant and land speculator, had once served his local parish as a preacher, and he saw education as a logical extension of religious life. Yet he was an eminently practical man: he had sought no lasting vocation in the ministry, had married to advantage, and had amassed a large fortune. He left his money to educational institutions that met his ideal of service to God and man—the two Phillips Academies, Dartmouth, and Princeton. His own alma mater, Harvard, received nothing because of what he considered its drift toward religious liberalism.

Shortly after his arrival in Exeter, John married the widow of Nathaniel Gilman. He opened a profitable lumber yard and hardware store facing Water Street with its own wharf on the river front. He added to his capital when he married another wealthy widow, the wife of a local physician, after his first wife died in 1765.

Farm lands acquired through marriage and purchase became the basis of his giving. Open-handed though he was, John Phillips had a reputation for constant attention to hard work and to the demands of religion. Tithing and philanthrophy were important forms of Christian service to him. He contributed generously to Eleazer Wheelock's school for Indian boys that grew into Dartmouth College, which he served devotedly as a trustee. A third of his estate went to the support of Phillips Academy and most of his remaining fortune to the Phillips Exeter Academy, the largest amount of money ever given to a private school at the time.

Phillips hoped to begin classes in 1781 when the state charter was granted, but it was not until suitable property was found on what is now Tan Lane in 1783 that the school formally opened. (It is said that if a landowner in Kingston hadn't been concerned that the boys might plunder his peach orchard, Phillips might have located there and hence the Phillips Kingston Academy.) The ideals that formed this academy and the principles that guided it were similar to those of the academy he and Samuel Phillips created in Andover. The constitutions of both proclaim the blessings of virtue and the dangers of vice, and both speak eloquently of the necessity of combining goodness with knowledge—"goodness without knowledge is weak and feeble, yet knowledge without goodness is dangerous" and that "both united form the noblest character and lay the surest foundation of usefulness to mankind."

Although the founder dreamed of a school that would provide the nation with an intellectual elite of strong moral fiber, he wanted its students to represent the entire population. Costs were to be kept to a minimum and scholarships made available to those who wanted an education but could not afford it. The original scheme of free tuition proved a greater burden than the endowment could carry, and in 1802 the trustees instituted a charge of $2.00. By 1870 it was still only $45. John Phillips left to his academy a democratic legacy and an estated valued at more than $65,000. Mrs. Phillips relinquished all claims so that Exeter could fully benefit from his estate, but she did receive a living allowance. The trustees later increased it somewhat and also gave her a cow. Andover, not to be outdone, also sent a cow.

The Academy's reputation for providing first-rate education at minimum cost grew steadily. To some, Exeter became entirely too democratic. In the 1840s, as the slavery question grew into a divisive issue, four boys from Kentucky withdrew when the Principal, Gidean Soule, refused to dismiss a black student. Exeter received boys at a crucial time in their lives and introduced them to others of a wide variety of backgrounds. Many formed friendships without concern for family background or social position.

Exeter's First Century

The Academy opened its doors in 1783 to 56 boys under the tutelage of the first Preceptor, William Woodbridge. Things did not go smoothly. Woodbridge was stern in his requirements for religious observance, calling the students to prayers before sunrise and again at sundown. Only boarding houses that would support this regime were approved by him and the trustees. At the end of five years Woodbridge resigned in frustration; enrollment had fallen to 13.

John Phillips selected a graduate of Phillips Academy, Benjamin Abbot, as his successor. He was given the title Principal as opposed to Preceptor and thus became the first Principal of the Academy. Phillips made a remarkably fortuitous choice, for Abbot gave Exeter outstanding leadership for half a century. He was as demanding as Woodbridge about assignments and attendance at worship, but he communicated a different spirit.

Benjamin Abbot knew how to deal with boys. He knew what went on inside them and operated according to a philosophy that worked with, rather than against, their nature. He seldom lectured them on their behavior. Rather, he set the example of a gentleman, always tipping his hat to every boy he met on the path outside. The impact on the students quickly became apparent. They were ashamed not to be open and honest with him. He could instill fear and impose punishment that required all niceties to be put aside. He allowed no quarrel or discussion, no resistance or escape. But once done, he did not linger over the matter nor allow the student to brood over his sins.

There was a love and respect for boys that may have been the key to Abbot's success. At the same time he believed that the burden of education rested essentially upon the shoulders of the student himself. Indeed, Abbot is credited with coining a phrase associated with Exeter education ever since: "the student must bear the laboring oar." Abbot also believed in a sense of order that freed the student from elaborate rules and restrictions. Gideon Soule, who followed Abbot, carried this one step further when he took charge in 1838. He reduced all previous regulations to one powerful statement: "the Academy has no rules—until they are broken."

In 1794, under the personal supervision of John Phillips, the second Academy building was constructed. It was a handsome example of the Georgian style that has long prevailed at the school. Abbot's combined classroom and office was on the first floor and was the center of life at the Academy. Descriptions of it suggest extreme austerity. There was only a clock in the corner and an iron stove in the middle. Abbot sat in a pulpit at one end of the room and listened to recitation given from a long bench enclosed in a pew along the wall. The atmosphere was somewhat confusing because loud recitations were being given at the same time that others were trying to study at their desks.

One of Dr. Abbot's students was Daniel Webster. Webster came to Exeter when he was fourteen from a modest rural background. Like other new boys before him and since, he was overpowered by the others who seemed to have seen so much of the world and to know so much more than he. He boarded with Squire Clifford at the "Gilman Garrison." It is said there was a problem at the dining table, where Webster would sit with a utensil clenched upright in each fist waiting for the food to be served. Sensing the delicacy of the problem, Clifford later arranged for one of the other boarders to do likewise and then permit Clifford to correct him rather than the new boy. One of Webster's teachers was Joseph Buckminster, always referred to as Mr. Buckminster by Webster in his correspondence, although Webster was fourteen and the latter but twelve. Despite the long days and heavy workload at the Academy, when classes were over in August, Dr. Abbot held "Exhibitions," a week of festivities that involved trustees, townspeople, and the students' families. Recitations, singing, and oratory terminated in a large picnic on the last day under the trees by the river.

Gideon Soule, the second Principal of the Academy, served from 1838 until 1873. He was deeply rooted in New England and married the great grand-daughter of the founder of the community of Exeter, Rev. John Wheelwright. Soule had studied at the Academy under Abbot and had picked up many of his ways. The boys respected Soule and seldom abused the confidence he had in them. One story involves a theft of several gates from homes in the town. The townspeople complained and asked that Soule call in the police. Soule decided otherwise. After evening prayers he talked about gentlemanly conduct and the importance of correcting any injury that one gentleman might have done to another as soon as possible. Later he noticed boys moving across the yard in the darkness bearing the gates back to their owners.

Soule believed in emphasizing a deep sense of honor and obligation, and in seeing that boys learned this in living rather than by lectures. It was in this context that he eliminated John Phillips' original rules of conduct and declared that there were no rules until they were broken. This was a bold move in 1838. Many schools were still operating under layers of restrictions over a hundred years later. Soule required only that the students be in their rooms by seven o'clock.

Soule made two other fundamental changes: in 1857 the trustees accepted a report prepared by Joseph Hoyt, a mathematics teacher, which recommended that the instructors should be recognized as a faculty and be in charge of running the daily affairs of the school. It was thus that much of the power of the trustees and the Principal was handed over to those more familiar with day-to-day events. The following year the trustees voted that all students could be excused from the Academy except during classes. Exeter was not a place for boys who needed constant surveillance. No longer were students required to do their lessons in a study hall under the eye of a preceptor. The individual student became responsible for his own success or failure, receiving the cherished privilege of studying on one's own time and building the self reliance that would be required in life later. *Huc venite pueri et viri sitis* — "hither come boys that they may become men" — was Soule's motto.

During Soule's administration, Exeter began its gradual conversion into a boarding school. The experiment was initially tried with the purchase and renovation of the building that originally housed the Williams Publishing Company. Its success led to the construction of Abbot Hall in 1855, the trustees feeling the students should not all have to fend for themselves in town.

In Soule's final year at Exeter, the third Academy building was erected, replacing the 1794 structure the school had outgrown. The architects were instructed to reproduce the building in its original Georgian style, but unfortunately, like all good architects, they proceeded to improve the design and bring it up-to-date. The date was 1872, the style was Victorian, and the attempt to blend the two resulted in an extraordinarily ugly building that stood as an embarrassment to the Academy until it mercifully burned to the ground in 1914.

One of the students at the Academy during Soule's principalship was Abraham Lincoln's son, Robert. Lincoln was a candidate for the presidency when the boy matriculated in 1860. Robert had tried to enter Harvard and after being turned down, attended Exeter for a year. His father wanted to visit him in New Hampshire, but the trip was a long one from Illinois. He therefore waited until receiving an invitation to speak in the East. One came from the Plymouth Church in Brooklyn.

But the Plymouth Church elders grew nervous when they realized that Lincoln would be allowed to talk on any subject of his choosing and were about to cancel the invitation when the Young Men's Central Republican Union of New York stepped in and arranged for him to speak at the Cooper Union. Lincoln's famous speech focused on the right of the federal government to control slavery. It was well received and given wide coverage in the New York press. Lincoln made the trip to Exeter, and soon other New England towns were inviting him to stop off on his way back from New Hampshire. Amos Tuck and other leaders of the newly-formed Republican Party encouraged his candidacy and Lincoln emerged from his first New England trip as a strong presidential contender. The momentum that began with a trip to visit his son carried through to the Chicago convention, with New England being one of his strongest supporting regions. Robert also prospered in the Northeast and entered Harvard the following year.

The Academy faculty at the time was dominated by strong personalities. In 1858 George Wentworth returned to Exeter and was joined by Bradbury Cilley the following year. Both were Exeter graduates who had entered Harvard as sophomores and roomed together. Both were to be strong forces in leading the Academy from its strict devotion to the classics toward a more modern curriculum. "Bull" Wentworth was big and bright. He was careless about his appearance but not about what he was thinking. And he could be tender. One night he carried a young scholarship boy, Thomas Lamont '88, down four flights of Gorham Hall stairs, placed him in a heated carriage, drove him to his own home, and carried him up to bed sick with scarlet fever. Lamont said later that Wentworth had a big brain but a bigger heart. The scholarship boy who arrived with nothing later became the head of J. P. Morgan and Company.

Rebirth of the Academy

Unfortunately, the easy rapport that developed between faculty and students at the end of the nineteenth century contributed to a relaxation in its standards, and many students had to be asked to leave. With a falling reputation the Academy attracted even fewer boys who were serious about their studies. Soule's successors were unable to reverse the situation. Professors Wentworth and Cilley dominated three short-term Academy Principals between 1873, when Soule retired, and 1895. It was not until the trustees stepped in and forced Wentworth's resignation while he was conveniently traveling in Egypt that a revival of the school was possible. The man who took the leadership of Exeter in 1895 proved one of the great educators of the early twentieth century, for it was he who turned the Academy into a great national boarding school.

Harlan Page Amen came from Sinking Spring, Ohio. He attended local schools and worked in the town bookshop but soon realized that to rise in the world he needed a better education. Friends of his employer suggested Exeter and, with their encouragement, he went. As a scholarship boy he was forced to earn his way, and he gained a reputation for diligence. After graduating from Exeter in 1875 and from Harvard in 1879, he went to teach at Riverview Academy in Poughkeepsie. When approached by the trustees of Exeter to become their next Principal, he laid down his conditions: that he should have their support in raising salaries and the tuition charge, in hiring new teachers, in dismissing students who were not working, and in building dormitories. He accepted a salary of $5,000, half of what he had been earning as an instructor in Poughkeepsie.

Most men would not have found such an offer very attractive, but Amen saw something in the Academy that was worth saving, something that distinguished it from the other New England academies that were foundering and disappearing. He recognized that residential schools on the English model, notably Groton and St. Paul's, were in great demand, and that Exeter must house, feed, and discipline its students if it were to fulfill the mission that its founder and benefactors had always intended for it. He was not a scholar, nor was he good at public speaking, athletics, or finances. But he was modest, earnest, and indefatigable. He was the inspiration that the students and faculty really needed. Amen was hardly an Olympian god — he did not have the time for that. He worked. Often he would toil in his office until the early hours of the morning before going home to a cold bath, breakfast, and then back for chapel before 8:00.

Dr. Amen traveled long distances to interview prospective students and faculty. In a sense he had to, because the student body had become filled with older boys who looked upon Exeter as a finishing point, not a preparation for college. Half of the student body was expelled at a time when the school could not easily afford such a loss. But gradually Amen managed to increase the enrollment.

He spared no time or expense in building up a strong faculty. He knew that neither imposing buildings nor an extensive campus could make a school great. It was essential to have strong, well-trained leaders of boys. Dr. Amen considered teaching at the secondary level just as important as at the college level, because anything that went wrong at the former could rarely be corrected at the latter. He also felt that although the intellectual challenges might not be as great, certainly the emotional ones were far greater. And he encouraged his faculty to share the lives of the students.

Under Amen, daily preparation was simply expected of all students. How one learned was up to the individual and was part of the education process, but reasonable effort had to be made. Otherwise the student was asked to go elsewhere. Once enrolled, the Academy respected the student as a man of honor to be trusted.

There was, however, a continuing problem with discipline. Amen saw that in many instances the problem was not the physical energy in the boys but finding a proper outlet for it. Class dinners had become a problem. Members of another class had been known to abduct the speaker of the evening, and occasionally strange malodorous concoctions from the chemistry lab were tossed in through open windows while the dinner was in progress. Riots and class fights were often overdramatized by the Boston newspapers, but they did occur and were giving the Academy a bad name. Amen's solution was to establish an arduous athletic program.

The program was designed to allow all boys to participate in a variety of sports and at a variety of levels so that each one could experience some degree of success. There were no rules for eligibility then and there are none today. In many respects the present program is patterned after that of the classroom. Given enough choice and levels of competence to be associated with, no student has to feel at the bottom.

Dr. Amen seemed to know every boy personally and tried to make each one feel that he was his best friend—especially the scholarship students. Often he would lend them money out of his own pocket. Dr. Amen died in 1913, the day after the school savored its first football victory over Andover in eight years—an event he had long waited for.

A Forgotten Boy named Harkness

Amen's successor, Lewis Perry, came to Exeter from Williams College in the summer of 1914. The main classroom building, the Victorian Gothic monstrosity of the previous century, had burned to the ground. However, Exeter's scholastic position was strong after eighteen years of reconstruction under Amen's steady leadership. Dr. Perry had studied at Lawrenceville and Williams. When he came to Exeter, he was at once struck by the democracy of the school. It far overshadowed anything he had ever experienced before. There was no sham or pretense about anyone or anything, and it was an atmosphere in which he enjoyed working for the next thirty years.

Lewis Perry had a tremendous fund of good will and a capacity for friendship that proved to be of immeasurable importance. Amongst his closest friends was Edward Harkness with whom he shared a passion for the theater. During his long association with John Rockefeller and Standard Oil, Harkness amassed a fortune that he shared with educational institutions, including his alma mater, Yale. But he had never discussed Exeter's needs with Perry in any serious way until the 1920s. In 1929 he asked Perry what Exeter would do to provide the finest education imaginable if money were no object. How, he wanted to know, could each student in a class be given the maximum opportunity to develop his own powers in competition with others? Perry formed a committee to answer Harkness's question. At first they submitted plans to help Exeter sustain its traditional notions—and Harkness rejected them all. He wanted something of a fundamentally different nature.

The committee soon realized that what Harkness wanted was a plan to give more attention to the individual student in order that he not be lost and forgotten as Harkness himself felt he had been at school. The plan that unfolded was as simple as it was radical: no more than twelve students in a class, with everyone sitting around a table. Until that time the instructor stayed on a platform, elevated and removed from the students who sat in rows. By gathering the class around the table this barrier was struck down and a greater willingness to participate was created. Both the teacher and the student were able to benefit because of the atmosphere of free and open communication. And of course there were no back rows for hiding anymore.

The Harkness Plan, simple in concept but expensive in implementation, is one of the reasons why Exeter is what it is today. The tutorial-like method required many new teachers. The overall plan also called for new classroom buildings, dining halls, and a fund for sabbatical leaves for the faculty.

Edward Harkness made his pledge in 1929 for all the money that would be required, and he honored his pledge despite the stock market collapse and the ensuing Depression. By 1935 the Academy had an enrollment of seven hundred boys and a faculty of eighty. The inauguration of the Harkness Plan revolutionized learning at Exeter. And the plan's success was due in large measure to Perry's great Dean of the Academy, Wells Kerr, for whom the Academy was both home and family for twenty-three years. He believed first and foremost in integrity and least of all in mischief. (One student later remarked that he did not know of anyone who could leap into a towering rage from a standing start sooner than Dean Kerr.) Kerr retired in 1953 and shortly thereafter the First Academy Building, which had been returned to a spot near its original location and restored, was named for him *(14)*.

The Post-War Years

After serving more than a decade as history teacher, coach, and dormitory adviser, William G. Saltonstall '24 represented and embodied both Exeter and New England at their best. A descendent of original Puritan settlers, he had attended Milton Academy and Exeter and was a tenth generation graduate of Harvard; he was a scholar and teacher greatly loved by his students; and he had been a fine athlete and a skilled sailor. Under his guidance, the Academy grew in fame and reputation during seventeen of the most satisfactory years in its history. In 1963 Saltonstall resigned to enter public service as head of the Peace Corps in Nigeria.

Richard Day arrived the following year, with Ernest Gillespie acting as transitional head. Under Day there were ambitious additions to the facilities — new dormitories to accommodate an extra two hundred students, a magnificent library, and greatly enlarged physical education facilities. The largest capital campaign ever carried out by a secondary school, the introduction of programs of study in Europe and of service internship in Washington, and a successful shift to coeducation marked the 1970s and the Day administration as perhaps the most innovative in the Academy's long history.

As Phillips Exeter Academy approaches its bicentennial, it continues to adhere with remarkable fidelity to the hopes and dreams of its founder. Under its present Principal, Stephen G. Kurtz, historian and former dean of Hamilton College, the faculty, trustees, and alumni reaffirm the ideal of a nationally representative and democratic school. The Academy stands in the forefront of the world's great secondary schools yet remains deeply rooted in the traditions and mores of rural New England.

The Thompson Science Building (1931)

Above: Merrill Hall in the Ford Quadrangle (1932)
Opposite: Phillips Hall (1932)

Above: The Lamont Gallery (1903) and Jeremiah Smith Hall (1931)
Opposite: The Thompson Science Building from Tan Lane (1931)

Above: Soule and Peabody Halls (1893, 1896)
Opposite: The Elm Street Dining Center (1970)
and Peabody Hall (1896)

Opposite: Hoyt and Soule Hall, (1903, 1893) and Abbot Hall (1855)
Above: Amen Hall (1925)

Afterglow

I would never call Exeter a jewel, and certainly during my years there it seemed to have lots of rough edges. But it smoothed some of *my* rough edges, and added facets to my knowledge and values in a way I didn't appreciate at the time.

Richard C. Marcus '56
Chairman, department store chain

Jeremiah Smith Hall (1931)

PEA's physical appearance

As a student in the late twenties, I gave little thought to how the Academy looked; it was enough to discover how one survived there. Yes, there were some memorably ugly spots—the heating plant and coal piles behind the Academy building, the ungainly former hat factory that housed the faculty club.

Today things are cleaned up and there are many new and often functionally beautiful additions. But Exeter has long stood for a certain rough no-nonsense in all matters and beauty is not its *first* claim to fame.

Bradford Bachrach '29
Photographer

Above: Gorham Hall (1851)
Opposite: The Exeter Inn (1932) and Wentworth,
Webster, and Dunbar Halls (1925, 1912, 1908)

Above: Along Front Street
Opposite: Merrill and Wheelwright Halls (1932, 1934)

Overview

From Cambridge I was driven along a snowy road that was lovely in the diminishing light to the village of Exeter, where there is a famous school in which I spent the night. Here I found what seemed to me to be the happiest sort of life that man can live: the scholastic life in which there is neither poverty nor wealth, in which older men continuously come in contact with waves of youth. I shall remember forever that small village in snow, with elm trees planted lavishly along its streets.

St. John Ervine
The Observer, November 11, 1928

Democracy

Phillips Exeter was a new and far wider world, boys there from all over the country, a truly national school as it has always been. It was, fortunately for me, thoroughly democratic. The fact that I had no money to spend was never a handicap, socially or in any other way. Just as many of the school leaders were scholarship boys as not. So I readily settled down in a congenial atmosphere.

Thomas W. Lamont 1888
Investment banker

Above: The Lamont Infirmary and Lamont Hall (1922)
Opposite: Ewald Hall (1969)

Snow

Not long afterward, early even for New Hampshire, snow came. It came theatrically, late one afternoon; I looked up from my desk and saw that suddenly there were big flakes twirling down into the quadrangle, settling on the carefully pruned shrubbery bordering the crosswalks, the three elms still holding many of their leaves, the still-green lawns. They gathered thicker by the minute, like noiseless invaders conquering because they took possession so gently. I watched them whirl past my window—don't take this seriously, the playful way they fell seemed to imply, this little show, this harmless trick.

It seemed to be true. The school was thinly blanketed that night, but the next morning, a bright, almost balmy day, every flake disappeared. The following weekend, however, it snowed again, then two days later much harder, and by the end of that week the ground had been clamped under snow for the winter.

from *A Separate Peace*
by John Knowles '45

The Academy Building Quadrangle *(above and preceding)*

The Academy Library (1971), above and following pages

Choice

Exeter is like a library. There are certain initial procedures for its usage, but from that point on, every shelf is available to the student. Once these procedures are met, there is no longer a need for a large "quiet" sign. The rules are instinctively understood. Drawer upon drawer of catalogue cards remind us that we have only dipped our toe.

Ralph L. Levy '38
Television and film director

The former Davis Library (1912), now the Davis Student Center

Latin struggle

One looks back at Exeter Latin as somewhat of an ordeal, a sort of trial by battle with the rigid difficulties of Roman grammar and syntax. Yet, there is also nostalgia for the remembered struggle, and pride for having survived it.

> Francis T.P. Plimpton '17
> Partner, New York law firm

Individualism

Unlike schools established after the Civil War for the sons of the new millionaires, Exeter and Andover were the last frontiers of plain living and high thinking, where the respect for things of the mind and for individualism carried on the tradition of 18th century New England.

Dwight MacDonald '24
Author

Classroom excellence

Although there was competition, I soon came to feel that I was part of a friendly group quite representative of what was best in the country. There was no Exeter type. But there was a common desire to excel in the classroom. There were brilliant students; there were slow ones; of laggards there were few. All felt an odd pride in Exeter. We wanted to belong, but belong to a school which we all felt was no place for the boy who lacked scholastic ability or who needed to be prodded and supervised.

Fritz W. Krebs '08
Steel company executive

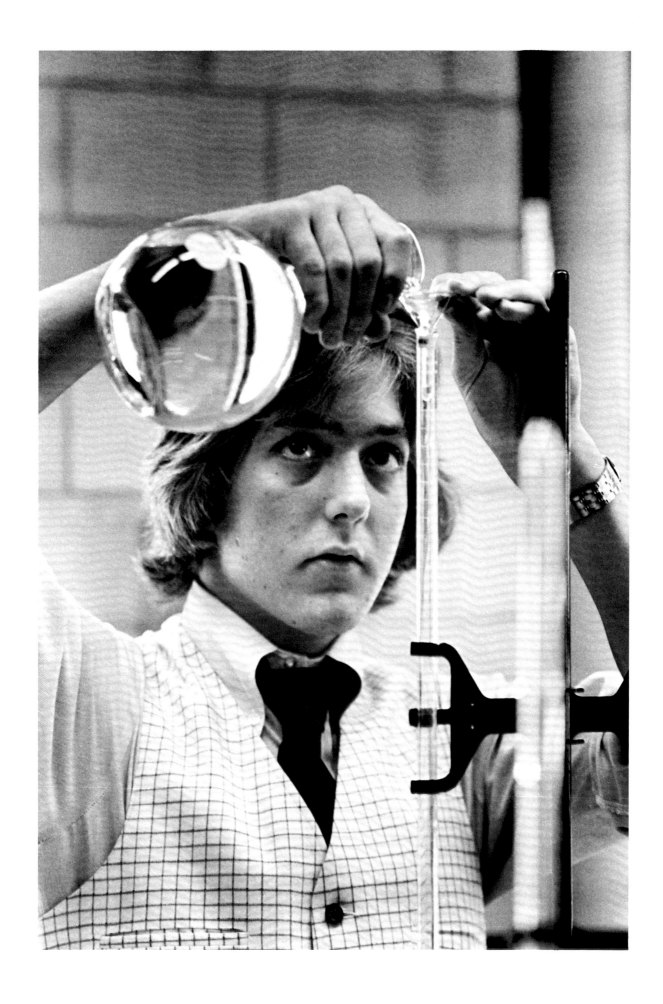

Respect

I can still remember, very vividly, the delight with which I gradually realized that I had, so to speak, been handed an entire new world, where books were as important as football, where brains were as well thought of as muscles, and where all sorts of useless things commanded respect, including myself. For I proved to be almost entirely useless, and must often have been the despair of the patient men who tried to drum the elements of science and mathematics into my head; and yet I was never given up for lost, for which I am grateful.

John R.A. Nash II '56
Educator, author

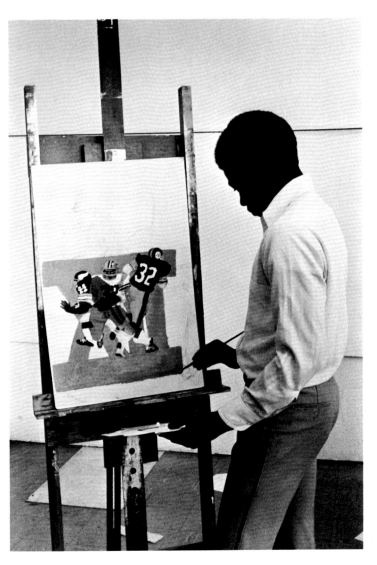

Responsibility

When I entered as a very small, frightened little fat boy of thirteen, Exeter seemed too big and utterly impossible. By the time I was graduating, three years later, Exeter seemed to me to be very wonderful, and I was very much at home. It was, for me, a concrete demonstration of that old phenomenon of having responsibility thrust upon you before you had proved you really deserved it and then discovering that you could live up to the requirements and expectations.

Calvin H. Plimpton '35
President and Dean, medical college

A new world

After being in a girl's school in Boston for five years with the same forty classmates, going to Exeter was like finding myself in a new world. I met people who were very different from those I'd known. With this came an interest in new subjects and sports which I had not experienced before.

Chloe J. Gavin '72
Law school student

Facing failure

Throughout those years I was not trying to analyze Exeter's
method of educating us; I was only trying to survive it.

Neil MacNeil '41
News commentator

Dear Son

You are now at a most important period of your life, my dear son, soon growing up to be a young man and a boy no longer, and I feel a great anxiety for your success and happiness...

Avoid all evil company and every temptation, and consider that you have now left your father's house and gone forth to improve your own character — to prepare your own mind for the part you are to lead in life. All that can be done for you by others will amount to nothing unless you do much for yourself.

Daniel Webster 1796
in a letter to his son, Edward,
upon entering the Academy in 1834

Coping

Each one of us has had his life profoundly influenced by some person, traumatic event or unusual opportunity. In my case it was Phillips Exeter Academy. I came here out of the Midwest, young, undeveloped, unsure of myself and frightened. I knew no one when I arrived and received nothing but D's my first term. Life at the Academy was lonely, difficult and unhappy. Yet it was an experience for which I have ever remained grateful. Exeter taught me how to cope with my society. And above all, it taught me how to use my mind.

John W. Nason '22
College president (retired)

No rules

Upon our checking in at PEA, they said to us restless youths, "There are no rules here until they are broken." To this day I like the implication of that aphorism — that a boy of fourteen or fifteen has the sense to know the difference if not between all that's right and all that's wrong, at least between what he reasonably might want to get away with and what he cannot. This is the great compliment that Exeter pays to its youth. It has more lasting meaning than the winning of prizes for athletic prowess or scholastic sharpness.

E. Blair Bolles '29
Manufacturing company adviser

Independence

It is true, what Exeter has often proclaimed, that the Academy is willing to permit boys maximum freedom in order that they might find their own way. This is a great blessing and one of the most important characteristics of the school. Next to parents, teachers suffer most from the temptation to play God with children. Although we had to study hard, it was obviously true that we were not possessed beyond our limits and that we had free time.

William M. Dietel '45
President, non-profit foundation

Work

Students studied if they wished to; but they were not forced to. Some got away without doing very much; some got expelled; but the majority learned that work does not harm and often explains matters that otherwise remain obscure, puzzling, and frustrating.

V. Lansing Collins '29
Foreign Service officer (retired)

163

Homesick

Young and alone I was put on a train in Illinois not knowing what to expect in far away New Hampshire. I found four seasons and Indians, but there the similarity ended. The experience made the difference in my life.

Alfred Brittain III '41
Chairman, New York bank

Democracy

At Exeter I was thrown in with boys from all over the country, from rich and poor families, where who a boy was or from what family he came was completely unimportant; the students accepted a boy or didn't only on the basis of his own character and behavior.

Walter A. Marting '36
Chairman, mining company (retired)

Discipline

It was the custom for all games of football that were taking place after classes in the yard to stop whenever the Principal or a senior member of the faculty passed through. On the first day of school in the fall one such game was under way and the kicker had just started towards the ball when he suddenly stopped. A new student, not realizing what was happening, thought the hesitation offered an excellent opportunity to show his abilities and proceeded to send the ball whizzing past the head of Dr. Soule, who at this point was crossing the yard. He writes:

"None of the boys 'made for it' as I expected they would do; but instead of that each one remained where he stood, and the dignified form of the Doctor halted, turned towards me, straightening up to his full height as he extended his long arm, and with his long, slim finger beckoned me to him. He was calm and dignified, and seemed to me very tall as I came near and looked up at him, while I, feeling myself in disgrace, seemed to lessen and dwindle proportionately. Very calmly, but without severity, he asked me if I was not a new pupil. I said that I was. Then he said, 'Take the ball and come home with me.' With all the meekness imaginable I picked up the ball, and followed the worthy Principal to his house, opposite the Academy grounds. What an interminable distance those few rods seemed to me! It is said that a drowning person in two minutes can live over again every incident in a long and checkered career; and you will not doubt the possibility of such a phenomenon if you have ever walked ten rods with a football under your arm, a new schoolmaster ten feet ahead, and the consciousness in your palpitating heart that you have committed a heinous crime against that glorious institution with which for a year you had been longing to be identified.

"I thought of all the mishaps of Tom Brown at Rugby, of the wretched Smike, and Oliver Twist, and by the time we had reached the Doctor's house, although I was not visibly black and blue from the rattan, I was inwardly black and blue from my harassing reflections. Once inside the door, however, the Doctor was most pleasant and affable. He assured me that he needed no explanation; that he saw just how the case stood; that he was sure I had intended no disrespect; that I was probably not aware that it was customary at the Academy for the pupils to check their sport for the minute or two required for the instructors to pass through the yard. This was all he said on that subject; then with a pleasant word or two on academy life in general, he with a knowing smile bade me take the ball back to the rest of the boys, and have as good a time as I knew how. With a lightened heart I hastened to rejoin my companions; and when I sent that ball back among them with the very highest kick that I could give, it did not even then rise to the level of my exalted opinion of the PHILLIPS EXETER ACADEMY and its gentlemanly way of disciplining its pupils."

George T. Tilden 1863
Architect

Facing failure

When I went home at Christmas, I was failing all my subjects but one. Dad said . . . I did not have to return unless I wished to. Something, however, told me I *had* to return if I was to live life satisfactory to myself from then on.

James F. Oates '17
Chairman, insurance company (retired)

Independence

You had friends when you wanted them, and you could be left alone when you wanted to be left alone.

Arthur M. Schlesinger, Jr. '33
Author, educator

Independence

Exeter allowed me the right to grow up in my own left-footed way, which was the one reason that had attracted me to the Academy in the first place.

Nathan C. Shiverick '47
Author

And now girls

Both my father and grandfather were not for coeducation at Exeter. They had enjoyed the all-male spirit and competitive atmosphere. But after my three years of fun and hard work, they knew that girls had added a new dimension to Exeter life.

Deborah Emery '79
College freshman

Trial run

Even though my earlier boyhood had been blessed by understanding, liberal minded parents, the feeling of freedom I experienced at Exeter was stimulating and challenging. Treating an underweight, skinny boy of 14 as if he did indeed have some judgment and common sense made that boy strive to do his very best within the limit of his capability. Exeter provided an invaluable trial run of life in the real world.

Jack R. Howard '28
Chairman, broadcasting company

Respect

Exeter wasn't very much fun for me when I was there but over the years I have become intensely loyal and feel very good having gone there.

John D. Rockefeller IV '54
Governor, West Virginia

Choice

I had in the Academy the excitement of choosing for myself how to spend a lot of time; the luxurious treat of breakfast at the grille *after* chapel some all-too-infrequent morning; wonderful Sunday afternoons with late fall sun and maybe a couple of hours on the "waters" (the term is used in its broadest sense) of the Exeter River. Shall I study now or goof-off? Even if I ended up studying *both* times, I had the feeling that I had had a choice.

James A. Fisher '38
Director, scientific instrument company

It doesn't change

Exeter has changed to the eye since I arrived as a nervous prep. But the enthusiasm of students in probing, questioning and exercising their intellect and sensitivities in fullest measure remains unchanged. One may not remember all the rules of trigonometry or the difference between a gerund and the gerundive, but the ability to use your mind, which Exeter faculty and students inspire so strongly, is an inexhaustible resource for a lifetime.

H. John Heinz '56
U.S. Senator

Shaping values

I think Exeter was second only to my parents in shaping my basic values. Although some of my *beliefs* have since changed, I shall always be very grateful for my four exciting years at the Academy.

John Cowles, Jr. '47
Publishing executive

Thought process

What can Exeter give each of its students to provide the capacity for leadership across a broad spectrum? An appetite for hard work, responsibility for organizing his own time and energy, the tested, basic skills with which to work at projects in writing or mathematics or science or in the arts — these are the most obvious. Less obvious are the educated man's skepticism, his rejection of fakery, his avoidance of conformity for its own sake, yet a willingness to accept conformity if its merits are there.

Brent M. Abel '33
Partner, San Francisco law firm

National high school

We are proud of our New England heritage, but increasingly desirous of attracting first-rate boys and girls from the most distant parts of the country and of the world. We believe that the loss a boy or girl suffers in leaving his family and community, though very considerable, is less than the gain resulting from life in a school like Exeter.

William Saltonstall '24
Principal, 1946-1963

Acknowledgements

Daniel Cook, John Emery, Edwin Frazer, Peter Hager,
Warren and Leona Henderson, James Lawrence,
Eliza Rees, Homer and Coverly Rees,

Blue Ribbon Sports, Inc., The Exeter Banking Company,
Indian Head National Bank, Wheelabrator-Frye, Inc.

Bradford Alden, Edward Baker, Anja Bankoski, Thomas Bates, Lynda Beck, Henry Bedford,
Nancy Belanger, Mrs. George Bennett, Hamilton Bissel, Mr. and Mrs. Charles Bickel, Valentine Bosetto,
Henry Bragdon, Richard Brinckerhoff, Robert Brownell, Miguel Buisán, Lawrence Bullard,
David Coffin, Donald Cole, Arthur Compton, Mrs. Allan Clarkson, Donald Chase,
William and Joanne Chase, Emma and John Crowe, William Damsell, DeVaux de Lancey,
James Del Buono, Edouard Desrochers, David Dimmock, Michael Dingman, Emile and Grace Dion,
Donald Doane, John Donnell, Margaret Duhamel, Donald Dunbar, Donald and Miriam Dunnan,
Edward and Mary Echols, Joyce Ernst, Reginald Frost, Robert Galt, Arthur Gilcreast, Robbins Gilman,
George Griffin, John Heath, John Hebert, John Herney, Norman Hess, James and Nancy Heyl,
Norman Hill, Lewis and Wendy Hitzrot, Colin Irving, Jeffrey Johnson, Daniel Jones, William Jones,
John Kane, Joyce Kennedy, Stephen and Jean Kurtz, Frederick Kusiak, Roy Ladner, Harriet Lundberg,
Ransom Lynch, Doris Maddox, Margaret Mann, Lorraine Marchand, Verna McGaughey,
Frederick McGowan, Johnston McLeod, Shirley Mensch, Nancy Merrill, Beverly Mills, Joyce Milner,
Ethel Mundy, Joseph Murphy, Olive Otis, Lillian Pineo, Andrew Polychronis, Margaret Rich,
Norman Ritter, Mrs. Percy Rogers, Grayce Rollins, Chester Rowe, Rosemond Roy,
Paul and Nancy Sadler, William Saltonstall, Winifred Sanborn, Kenneth Sargent, Alice Schmechel,
Edna Schneider, Donald and Judy Schultz, Doris Smart, Douglas Snow, Thomas Stephenson,
Neil Stone, Ben and Cathy Swiezynski, Charles Swift, Dudley Taft, Thomas Taft, Carol Taylor,
Elizabeth Terry, James Theisen, David and Jacqueline Thomas, Harris Thomas, Mary Thomas,
Dorothy Thorp, Viola Thurston, Eleanor Tremallo, André Vernet, John Warren, William White,
Robert Woodell, Valerie Woods.

Alling & Cory, Canfield Papers, Inc., Robert Burlen & Son, Inc., World Composition Services, Inc.,

Stevan Baron, James Beardsley, Avis Berman, Steven Borns, Richard Brown, Kenneth Cannon,
Lucy Carlborg, Kirtland Crump, Elaine Donnelly, Hoyt Evans, Robert Fragetti, Alan Frese, Jean Frey,
Earl Gardner, Charles Greensmith, William Hanashey, Patrick Koechlin, Rod Leprine, George Mazawey,
Thomas Mendecino, Michael Minnicino, Beverly Nadelson, Thomas O'Brien, Sidney Rapoport,
Ronald Raye, Lee Salem, BeeGee Sciancalepore, Henry Smith-Miller, Bruce Zahor, Ruth Zimmerman.

The quotation from John Knowles' *A Separate Peace* (Macmillan & Co., 1959) is reprinted by permission
of Curtis Brown, Ltd.